DATE DUE

The U.S. Constitution

The U.S. Constitution

Dennis Brindell Fradin

Marshall Cavendish
Benchmark

New York

Dedication

For my daughter-in-law, April Ann Burch Fradin, with love

Marshall Cavendish Benchmark
99 White Plains Road
Tarrytown, NY 10591
www.marshallcavendish.us

Text and maps copyright © 2008 by Marshall Cavendish Corporation
Maps by XNR Productions

Library of Congress Cataloging-in-Publication Data

Fradin, Dennis B.
The U.S. Constitution / Dennis Brindell Fradin.
p. cm. — (Turning points in U.S. history)
Includes bibliographical references and index.
ISBN-13: 978-0-7614-2036-1
1. United States. Constitution—Juvenile literature. 2. United
States—Politics and government—1775–1783—Juvenile literature. 3. United
States—Politics and government—1783–1789—Juvenile literature.
4. Constitutional history—United States—Juvenile literature. I. Title. II. Series.

E303.F76 2007
973.3'18—dc22

2006025348

Photo research by Connie Gardner

Cover Photo: Hulton Archive/Getty Images
Title Page: Peggy and Ronald Barnett/Getty Images

The photographs in this book are used by permission and through the courtesy of: *The Granger Collection:* 6, 14, 24, 32, 34;
Corbis: Poodles Rock, 8; Bettmann, 9, 28; Corcoran Gallery of Art, 10; *Getty Images:* Hulton Archive, 12; *Art Resource:* HIP, 15; Reunion des Musees
Nationaux, 18; National Portrait Gallery, Smithsonian Institution, 29; *North Wind Picture Archives:* 16, 20.

Time Line: North Wind Picture Archives

Editor: Deborah Grahame
Publisher: Michelle Bisson
Art Director: Anahid Hamparian

Printed in Malaysia
1 3 5 6 4 2

Contents

CHAPTER ONE: The Thirteen Colonies Become the United States 7

CHAPTER TWO: The Articles of Confederation 13

CHAPTER THREE: "Congress Must Be Invested with Greater Powers" 17

CHAPTER FOUR: The Constitutional Convention Opens 21

CHAPTER FIVE: "It Was Done by Bargain and Compromise" 25

CHAPTER SIX: "More Perfect Than Any Form of Government" 35

Glossary 40

Timeline 42

Further Information 44

Bibliography 46

Index 47

Settlers are shown loading tobacco onto ships in the James River, Virginia, during the 1600s.

CHAPTER ONE

The Thirteen Colonies Become the United States

England settled Virginia, its first North American colony, in 1607. It established Georgia, its thirteenth colony, in 1733. For many years Britain ruled its colonies peacefully.

In the 1760s Britain's relationship with its colonies worsened. Money was a big part of the problem. Britain owed an enormous amount of money to other countries. British lawmakers ordered that Americans help settle these debts by paying taxes on items ranging from paper goods to tea. Americans protested, sometimes violently. In December 1773, Massachusetts patriots dumped British tea into Boston Harbor. Today, this event is called the Boston Tea Party.

Patriots dressed as Indians dumped more than three hundred chests of tea into Boston Harbor.

Taxes were not the only reason the Americans rebelled. By the 1770s many colonists wanted to rule themselves, rather than continue to take orders from the Mother Country. However, Britain would not give up its thirteen colonies without a fight.

Colonists fire their guns at the British redcoats during the Battle of Lexington.

The Revolutionary War between Britain and the colonies began at Lexington, Massachusetts, on April 19, 1775. The next year, in July 1776, American leaders issued the **Declaration of Independence**. For a long time it looked like Britain's superior army and navy would put

An oil painting depicts George Washington before the Battle of Yorktown during the Revolutionary War.

down the revolt. But the Americans had two things in their favor. First, they were fighting on their home soil. Second, they had fine leaders. Army commander George Washington had strong military skills. Benjamin Franklin convinced France to fight on the Americans' side. With French aid, the United States won the Revolutionary War—and its independence—in 1783.

John Hancock was the first signer of the Declaration of Independence while serving as president of Congress.

CHAPTER TWO

The Articles of Confederation

In 1781 the United States adopted the **Articles of Confederation**. This document created a weak central government for the new country. Most Americans did not want their government to have much power. They were afraid that a strong central government would tax them and tell them what to do.

The government under the Articles of Confederation proved to be *too* weak, however. In fact, the government was helpless in almost every way in the country's early years. To start with, there was no president of the United States. The closest thing to a national leader—the president of Congress—had little power. Except for John Hancock of

A four-dollar banknote issued in Georgia in 1777.

Massachusetts, the presidents of Congress between 1776 and 1787 are mostly forgotten today.

The new country also lacked a permanent **capital**. Philadelphia, Pennsylvania, had been the national capital when the Declaration of Independence was issued in July 1776. Over the next nine years, the

A tin pattern for a silver dollar, issued in 1776.

capital was moved nine times. It went to Baltimore, Maryland; back to Philadelphia; to Lancaster, Pennsylvania (for a single day); to York, Pennsylvania; back again to Philadelphia; to Princeton, New Jersey; to Annapolis, Maryland; to Trenton, New Jersey; and to New York City.

Congress lacked authority to impose taxes, so it could only beg the states for funds. In a typical year, Congress asked for 8 million dollars. The states would send only one-twentieth of that amount—about $400,000. As a result, Congress could not pay all its bills.

The government had other problems. The country had no national money system. Instead, each state issued its own money. Since the money's value was different from place to place, doing business was confusing. The country had no national courts to settle disagreements between states or to rule on cases of nationwide importance. The government commanded such little respect that some states did not even bother to send **delegates** to Congress.

This busy street scene features Philadelphia's Independence Hall as it looked in 1776.

CHAPTER THREE

"Congress Must Be Invested with Greater Powers"

A series of events showed the colonists how badly they needed a stronger central government. In June 1783, as the war was ending, Congress was meeting at Independence Hall in Philadelphia. About one hundred American troops surrounded the building. The soldiers smashed windows and shouted that Congress had better hand over their pay. The congressmen did not have the funds to pay the troops. What did they do? They ran away to Princeton, New Jersey, which then became the U.S. capital.

Shays's Rebellion also showed the weakness of the central government. This revolt was led by Daniel Shays and other farmers in

James Madison

James Madison grew up at his family's Virginia plantation, Montpelier, which remained his lifelong home. In the 1770s Madison served in Virginia's revolutionary government. He helped write Virginia's first state **constitution** of 1776.

Madison was a leading figure at the Constitutional Convention of 1787. Many proposals from his Virginia Plan went into the new government's framework. Much of what we know about the convention comes from the notes that Madison took. Madison also wrote essays to help the Constitution win approval throughout America.

For all that he did, Madison is known as the Father of the Constitution. Later, from 1809 to 1817, Madison served as the fourth president of the United States.

James Madison (1751–1836)

Massachusetts. It lasted from the autumn of 1786 until 1787. The farmers were protesting high local taxes and laws that sent debtors to jail. The seven-hundred-man U.S. Army was not strong enough to stop the rebellion. Instead, the Massachusetts militia, or emergency troops, had to do it.

American leaders realized that the nation might collapse unless the government was strengthened. In May 1786 Charles Pinckney of South Carolina warned his fellow congressmen, "Congress must be invested with greater powers, or the federal government must fall. Congress [must] appoint a **convention** for that purpose." That autumn, in a letter to fellow Virginian James Madison, George Washington predicted that the government would topple "without some **alteration** in our political **creed**." Around that time, New Yorker Alexander Hamilton warned that "important defects in the system of the federal government" needed fixing.

In February 1787 Congress called for a convention to be held in Philadelphia that May. Each state was asked to send delegates to this meeting. The purpose of the meeting was to increase the power of the federal government.

George Washington is shown presiding over delegates at the 1787 Constitutional Convention.

CHAPTER FOUR

The Constitutional Convention Opens

Rhode Island, the smallest state, sent no delegates to the convention in Philadelphia. Little Rhody, as the state was nicknamed, feared that the large states would dominate a stronger central government. The twelve other states sent a total of fifty-five delegates to the convention. The convention opened on May 25, 1787. That day, George Washington was **unanimously** elected convention president.

Many of the delegates were well-known leaders. John Dickinson of Delaware, Ben Franklin and James Wilson of Pennsylvania, and William Livingston of New Jersey attended the convention. Also present were Abraham Baldwin of Georgia, Roger Sherman of Connecticut,

John Dickinson

John Dickinson (1732–1808) had an unusual career. He practiced law in Pennsylvania and Delaware and served in both colonies' legislatures. From 1781 to 1782 he was governor of Delaware, and from 1782 to 1785 he governed his other home state, Pennsylvania. For several weeks he governed both states at the same time!

Dickinson wrote the first draft of the Articles of Confederation. As a Constitutional Convention delegate, however, he knew that the country needed a stronger government. Although his name is on the Constitution as one of the thirty-nine Founders, Dickinson did not actually sign it. He left the convention early due to illness, but he arranged for fellow Delaware delegate George Read to sign for him. Dickinson's support for the Constitution helped Delaware and Pennsylvania become the first two states to ratify the document.

Nathaniel Gorham of Massachusetts, James McHenry of Maryland, and the cousins Charles Pinckney and Charles Cotesworth Pinckney of South Carolina. Other strong leaders were John Langdon of New Hampshire, James Madison and George Washington of Virginia, Alexander Hamilton of New York, and Hugh Williamson of North Carolina.

At first, many delegates just wanted to improve the Articles of Confederation. That method presented problems. To amend, or change, the articles, every state had to give its approval. Rarely did all thirteen states agree on anything. Besides, Rhode Island was not represented at the convention. The delegates made a historic decision. They would replace the Articles of Confederation with a new government framework. This new document became known as the **Constitution of the United States**.

The delegates also decided that the Constitutional Convention would work by **majority rule**. Each state would have one vote on each proposal. If a state had three delegates, two of them had to vote for a proposal for it to be approved. For a proposal to be placed in the Constitution, a majority of states had to approve it.

This painting shows the interior of the U.S. Congress House as it appeared in the early 1800s.

CHAPTER FIVE

"It Was Done by Bargain and Compromise"

The delegates quickly agreed on the basic kind of government the new Constitution would create. It would have three branches. The **legislative branch**, or Congress, would make laws. The **executive branch**, headed by a president, would make sure the laws were carried out. The **judicial branch** would make important legal decisions.

However, the delegates disagreed on many key points. For example, how many years should the president serve? Eight years, suggested one delegate. Others argued for a three-, four-, seven-, eleven-, or fifteen-year term of office. It was even proposed that the country have three presidents! Some wanted the president (or presidents) to be eligible, or

qualified, for reelection. Others disagreed with that idea.

How many houses of Congress should there be? And how many **legislators** should each state have? Virginia's delegates, led by James Madison, presented the Virginia Plan, or Large-State Plan. It proposed a two-house legislature: the U.S. House of Representatives and the U.S. Senate. The larger a state's population, the more representatives and senators it would have.

The delegates from the small states were strongly against that idea. It meant that states where many people lived, such as Virginia and Pennsylvania, would control Congress. The smaller states answered with the New Jersey Plan, or Small-State Plan. It proposed a one-house legislature in which each state would have an equal vote.

What about slavery? Some delegates wanted to outlaw slavery. Some delegates from the South, where slavery was growing, would have nothing to do with an antislavery constitution. There was another sticky question about the slaves. When counting a state's population, should slaves be counted as people or as property? To some delegates, slaves were obviously people. To others, slaves were the property of their owners. This was an important issue, for a state's population might determine how many representatives it had in Congress. It might also determine how much money a state would have to pay in taxes.

The arguing sometimes grew so heated that delegates threatened to

The Constitution's Main Author

All the delegates helped create the ideas in the Constitution. However, a Pennsylvanian was mainly responsible for the document's actual wording. Gouverneur Morris (1752–1816) was born in present-day New York City. His first name honored his mother, whose maiden name was Sarah Gouverneur. Morris became a lawyer. From 1778 to 1779 he represented New York at the Continental Congress. He was asked to write many papers because of his way with words.

Shortly after losing his bid for reelection to Congress in 1779, Morris moved to Philadelphia. Not long after the move, he lost his left leg in a carriage accident and was given a wooden leg. He did not let it stop him from horseback riding, canoeing, and even taking ten-mile walks. While representing Pennsylvania at the Constitutional Convention, Morris made 173 speeches—more speeches than any other delegate. He also was the main author of the written text of the Constitution.

walk out. In mid-July it appeared that the convention might break up without producing a constitution. Jacob Broom, a delegate from Delaware, leaped to his feet and warned that they must control their tempers. Broom convinced the delegates to work out their disagreements and helped to save the convention.

Benjamin Franklin signed both the Declaration of Independence and the U.S. Constitution.

Ben Franklin was the oldest delegate, at age eighty-one. He gave his fellow delegates some advice by telling a story. When making a table, said Ben, sometimes a carpenter must cut a little from one board and a little from another board to fit the pieces together. "In like manner," he concluded, everyone at the convention "must part with some of their demands" if they were to accomplish anything. In other words, they must compromise. This was exactly what they did.

The delegates made a major compromise about the legislature. It was called the Connecticut Compromise because Roger Sherman of Connecticut proposed it. The Connecticut Compromise called for a two-house Congress. A state's membership in the House of Representatives would be based on population, but every state would have an equal number of senators. That way the large and small states would each get some of what they wanted. The Connecticut Compromise was approved. As a result, each state has two

Roger Sherman

The man who proposed the Connecticut Compromise was born in Massachusetts. After becoming a shoemaker, Roger Sherman moved to Connecticut at the age of twenty-two. He reportedly walked nearly 150 miles to his new home with his tools on his back. Sherman became a lawyer, lawmaker, and judge. He was also the father of fifteen children, the most of any of the Founders. Sherman was one of only six men who signed both the Declaration of Independence and the U.S. Constitution.

Fittingly, Sherman served in both houses of the nation's legislature in his later years. He represented Connecticut in the House of Representatives from 1789 to 1791 and in the U.S. Senate from 1791 until his death.

Roger Sherman (1732–1808)

Patriotic Numbers and Names

William Livingston, a Founding Father from New Jersey, had seven sons and six daughters with his wife, Susanna French Livingston. Having thirteen children was good because that was the "number of the United States," Livingston said.

A Founder from South Carolina, John Rutledge, had seven sons and three daughters with his wife, Elizabeth Grimke Rutledge. The Rutledges named their tenth child States Rutledge as a living reminder that the nation was a union of states.

U.S. senators but anywhere from one to several dozen U.S. representatives.

The delegates decided that the nation would have one president elected to a four-year term. Delegates who wanted a longer term got something, too. It was decided that the president could be reelected any number of times.

Slavery was also a subject for compromise. Delegates agreed that Congress could outlaw bringing new slaves into the United States. However, Congress could not do this until 1808—twenty-one years in the future. Another compromise involved how to count slaves. For the purposes of counting the population, each slave would be counted as three-fifths of a person.

For four months, the delegates hammered out the Constitution point by point. They decided to establish a permanent capital, which turned out to be Washington, D.C. Could new states be added to the original thirteen? Yes, but a new state could not break away from another state without its consent. If state laws clashed with national laws, then the Constitution and federal laws were to be "the supreme law of the land."

What if Americans wanted to amend the Constitution? It could be done if three-fourths of the states approved. Finally, how would the Constitution go into effect? Delegates decided that the states would hold their own conventions to consider approving the document. If nine of the thirteen states approved it, the Constitution would become the nation's new framework of government.

The Constitution was signed on September 17, 1787—the last day of the meeting in Philadelphia. Thirteen of the fifty-five delegates had left the convention early and were unable to sign the document. Three men who disliked the Constitution refused to sign it. The thirty-nine men who signed the Constitution are called the **Founding Fathers**.

Nicholas Gilman, a Founder from New Hampshire, summed up how the Constitution had been created. "It was done by bargain and compromise," Gilman wrote to a friend. While realizing that the Constitution was not perfect, most of the Founders liked it overall.

The fourth and final page of the U.S. Constitution, featuring the signatures of the thirty-nine delegates.

George Washington, for example, called it "the best Constitution that can be obtained."

Still, the Constitution would not be anything at all unless nine states approved it. If that did not happen, the Articles of Confederation would remain the law of the land.

An illustration from the late 1700s shows people expressing enthusiasm for and confidence in the United States Constitution.

CHAPTER SIX

"More Perfect Than Any Form of Government"

In late 1787 the states began holding conventions to consider whether or not to approve the Constitution. Many people, called **Federalists**, favored the new Constitution. The leading Federalists included the men who had created and signed the document. For example, Hugh Williamson of North Carolina praised the Constitution as "more free and more perfect than any form of government that has ever been adopted by any nation."

No one knew if the required nine states would grant their approval. The Constitution also had many opponents. Called **Anti-Federalists**, these people believed that the new framework would give the central government too much power.

On December 7, 1787, Delaware became the first state to ratify, or approve, the Constitution. Over the next five months, Pennsylvania, New Jersey, Georgia, Connecticut, Massachusetts, Maryland, and South Carolina also ratified the document. Just one more state was needed to put the Constitution into effect.

New Hampshire held its convention in mid-1788. On June 21, by a narrow 57 to 47 vote, New Hampshire leaders approved the Constitution. With this vote, the U.S. Constitution replaced the Articles of Confederation as the law of the land.

Now came a new problem. What about Virginia, New York, North Carolina, and Rhode Island? Unless they ratified the Constitution, they were almost like foreign countries instead of part of the United States.

Just four days after New Hampshire became the ninth state, Virginia became the tenth by approving the Constitution. New York became the eleventh state in July 1788. In North Carolina and Rhode Island, many people felt that the Constitution did not protect citizens' basic rights. By 1789 the process of adding the first ten amendments to the Constitution was under way. Known as the **Bill of Rights**, these amendments protect such basic rights as freedom of religion and the right to a fair trial.

The creation of the Bill of Rights helped persuade North Carolina

Official Statehood

With the writing of the Declaration of Independence in 1776, the thirteen colonies became known as states. But when Americans use the word *states* today, however, they mean states under the Constitution. The former colonies became states in the modern sense on the day they ratified the Constitution. Here is when the thirteen former colonies approved the Constitution and achieved official statehood:

1. Delaware: Friday, December 7, 1787
2. Pennsylvania: Wednesday, December 12, 1787
3. New Jersey: Tuesday, December 18, 1787
4. Georgia: Wednesday, January 2, 1788
5. Connecticut: Wednesday, January 9, 1788
6. Massachusetts: Wednesday, February 6, 1788
7. Maryland: Monday, April 28, 1788
8. South Carolina: Friday, May 23, 1788
9. New Hampshire: Saturday, June 21, 1788
10. Virginia: Wednesday, June 25, 1788
11. New York: Saturday, July 26, 1788
12. North Carolina: Saturday, November 21, 1789
13. Rhode Island: Saturday, May 29, 1790

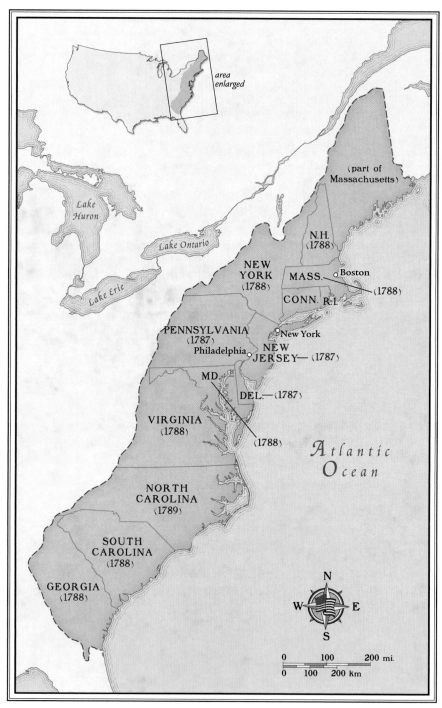

This map shows the thirteen colonies and the dates each approved the Constitution.

leaders to approve the Constitution in late 1789. And finally, on May 29, 1790, by the closest vote of all—34 to 32—Rhode Island became the last of the original thirteen states to approve the Constitution.

As the Founders signed the Constitution on September 17, 1787, Ben Franklin made a memorable comment. During the four-month-long meeting, George Washington had sat in a chair with a carved image of the sun on it. Ben had often asked himself whether the sun was intended to be setting or rising. The new Constitution gave him so much hope that he finally knew the answer.

"It is a rising sun!" Franklin said.

He was right. Since its adoption, more than two hundred years ago, the Constitution has guided the country through many rough times. Thanks to the Constitution, the United States has not just survived. It has become one of the most powerful and successful nations on Earth.

Glossary

alteration—A change.

Anti-Federalists—People who opposed the adoption of the Constitution in the late 1780s.

Articles of Confederation—The framework of government that was in force in the United States between 1781 and 1788.

Bill of Rights—The first ten amendments to the U.S. Constitution.

capital—The place where the laws for a nation or state are made.

constitution—A basic framework of government.

Constitution of the United States—The document, created in 1787 and in effect since 1788, that is the law of the land.

convention—A big meeting.

creed—A set of beliefs or guiding principles.

Declaration of Independence—The document, issued in 1776, announcing that the thirteen colonies had become the United States of America.

delegates—People who act on behalf of other people.

executive branch—The branch of government that enforces the law and commands the armed forces.

Federalists—People who favored the adoption of the Constitution in the late 1780s.

Founding Fathers (or Founders)—The thirty-nine men who signed the Constitution. Sometimes all the leaders in the country's early days are called the Founding Fathers.

judicial branch—The branch of government composed of courts and judges.

legislative branch—The branch of government that makes laws.

legislators—Men and women who make laws.

majority rule—A system by which decisions are made when more than half the people agree.

unanimously—With the vote or support of all people present.

Timeline

1607—Britain establishes Virginia, its first colony in North America

1733—Britain establishes Georgia, the last of its thirteen North American colonies

1773—During the Boston Tea Party, Americans protest the Mother Country's tax on tea by dumping British tea into Boston Harbor

1775—**April 19:** The American Revolution begins at Lexington, Massachusetts

1776—**July 4:** The Continental Congress approves the Declaration of Independence

1781—The United States adopts the Articles of Confederation

1783—Americans win the Revolutionary War

1786–1787—Shays's Rebellion shows the weakness of the central government

1607   *1776*   *1781*

1787—May 25: The Constitutional Convention opens in Philadelphia
September 17: Thirty-nine Founding Fathers sign the Constitution of the U.S.
December 7: Delaware becomes the First State by ratifying the Constitution

1788—June 21: The Constitution goes into effect when New Hampshire becomes the ninth state to ratify it

1790—May 29: Rhode Island becomes the last of the original thirteen states to approve the Constitution

1791—December 15: The Bill of Rights goes into effect

1887—September 17: One-hundredth anniversary of the signing of the Constitution

1987—September 17: Two-hundredth anniversary of the signing of the Constitution

1788

1791   1987

Further Information

BOOKS

Graves, Kerry A. *The Constitution: The Story Behind America's Governing Document*. Philadelphia: Chelsea House, 2004.

Morin, Isobel V. *Our Changing Constitution: How and Why We Have Amended It*. Brookfield, CT: Millbrook, 1998.

Nardo, Don. *The U.S. Constitution*. San Diego: KidHaven Press, 2002.

Teitelbaum, Michael. *The U.S. Constitution*. Chanhassen, MN: The Child's World, 2005.

National Archives Web page relating to the U.S. Constitution:
www.archives.gov/national-archives-experience/charters/constitution.html

A government-sponsored Web page about the Constitution for children
in grades three through five, with links:
http://bensguide.gpo.gov/3-5/documents/constitution/index.html

A government-sponsored Web page on the history of the Constitution
for children in grades six through eight, with links:
http://bensguide.gpo.gov/6-8/documents/constitution/background.html

A National Park Service Web site with biographical pages for each of the
signers of the Constitution:
www.cr.nps.gov/history/online_books/constitution/bioa.htm

Bibliography

Berkin, Carol. *A Brilliant Solution: Inventing the American Constitution.* New York: Harcourt, 2002.

Ferling, John E. *The First of Men: A Life of George Washington.* Knoxville: University of Tennessee Press, 1988.

McLaughlin, Andrew Cunningham. *The Confederation and the Constitution: 1783–1789.* New York: Harper & Row, 1905.

Morris, Richard B. *The Framing of the Federal Constitution.* Washington, DC: National Park Service, 1986.

Rutland, Robert A. *James Madison: The Founding Father.* New York: Macmillan, 1987.

Whitney, David C. *Founders of Freedom in America: Lives of the Men Who Signed the Constitution of the United States.* Chicago: Ferguson, 1965.

Index

Page numbers in **boldface** are illustrations.

maps, 38

army
    state militias, 19
    of United States, **9**, 17, 19
Articles of Confederation, 13–14,
    22, 23

Bill of Rights, 36–39
Boston Tea Party, 7, **8**
Broom, Jacob, 27

capital, 14–15, **16**, 17, 24, 31
citizens' rights, 36–39
colonies, 7, 13, **38**
    See also states
Congress
    and Articles of Confederation,
        13–17
    in Constitution, **24**, 25, 26, 28–30
Connecticut Compromise, 28
Constitutional Convention of 1787
    delegates, 21–23
    disagreements, 25–30
    length, 39
    Madison role, 18, 26
    place and time, 21
    purpose, 19
    voting rules, 23
Constitution of the United States
    adoption, 18, 22, 31–39
    authorship process, 27, 31
    changes, 31, 36–39

effectiveness, 39
    signing, 22, 31, **32**, 38
courts, 15, 25

Declaration of Independence, 9, **12**,
    14, **16**
Dickinson, John, 22

Federalists, 35
Founding Fathers, 30, 31
France, 11
Franklin, Benjamin, 11, 21, 28, **28**,
    39

Georgia, 7, **14**
Gilman, Nicholas, 31
government power
    under Articles of Confederation,
        13–14, 17–19
    under Constitution, 25, 35
Great Britain, 7–11

Hamilton, Alexander, 19–23, **20**
Hancock, John, **12**, 13–14

Independence Hall, 16, 17

Livingston, William, 30

Madison, James, 18, **18**, 26
money, 7, **14**, 15, **15**, 17
Morris, Gouverneur, 27

New Jersey plan, 26
North Carolina, 36–39

patriotism, 30
Pinckney, Charles, 19
presidents, 13–14, 18, 25–26, 30

Revolutionary War, **9**, 9–11
Rhode Island, 21, 36–39
Rutledge, John, 30

Shays's Rebellion, 17–19
Sherman, Roger, 21, 28, 29, **29**
slavery, 26, 30
states
    addition of, 31
    adoption of Constitution, 22,
        31–39
    armies (militias), 19
    constitutional input, 23
    laws of, 31
    and money, 17
    size issue, 26
    statehood dates, 37, **38**

taxes, 7–8, 13, 15, 19

Virginia, **6**, 7, 18, 26
Virginia plan, 18, 26

Washington, George, **10**, 11, 19, **20**,
    21, 33, 39

About the Author

Dennis Fradin is the author of 150 books, some of them written with his wife, Judith Bloom Fradin. Their recent book for Clarion, *The Power of One: Daisy Bates and the Little Rock Nine*, was named a Golden Kite Honor Book. Another of Dennis's recent books is *Let It Begin Here! Lexington & Concord: First Battles of the American Revolution*, published by Walker. The Fradins are currently writing a biography of social worker and antiwar activist Jane Addams for Clarion and a nonfiction book about a slave escape for National Geographic Children's Books. Turning Points in U.S. History is Dennis Fradin's first series for Marshall Cavendish Benchmark. The Fradins have three grown children and three young grandchildren.